The Skull Man

and Other People with Cool Jobs

Nonfiction by Patrick Daley

SCHOLASTIC INC.

New York   Toronto   London   Auckland   Sydney
Mexico City   New Delhi   Hong Kong

Cover photograph © Bill Cramer

Photo credits

Pages 6-7: Philadelphia Inquirer/ Michael Bryant;

page 11: Frank Bender;

pages 14, 15: ©Bill Cramer Photography;

page 17: Courtesy Amy Weller;

pages 19, 21, 22: Courtesy Ben & Jerry's;

pages 27, 30: John Lei for Scholastic, Inc.;

pages 34, 38: Gerry Lewin for Scholastic, Inc.;

page 41: Bruce Thorson/ Statesman Journal;

pages 43, 45, 46, 49, 51: Zoological Society of San Diego.

Additional reporting for this book was done
by John DiConsiglio and Tod Olson.

Table of
Contents

Dear Reader,

Imagine this: You are at a big family dinner. Your Aunt Lucy is making her way across the room—right toward you. Yikes! Before you can dive behind the sofa, she grabs you. With a firm grip on your ear, she puts her face right in yours and says, "Honey, what do you want to do when you grow up?"

Of course, the quick and easy answer would be something like, "Oh, I want to be a teacher . . . or a firefighter . . . or a pilot."

That might be good enough to make Aunt Lucy go away. But what do you *really* want to do when you grow up? What if you don't want to be a teacher, or a firefighter, or a pilot? What if you want to take pictures . . . or ride trains . . . or feed animals . . . or hang out at an ice cream factory? What if you want to do something really odd, something almost no one else does? Or what if you have no idea what you want to do?

Hey! That's okay. You have lots of time to figure it out. And this book just might help! In these pages, you'll meet some people who have pretty wild jobs. You may want a job like one of theirs—or not! Either way, you'll probably find their jobs interesting. So, before Aunt Lucy corners you again, check out these careers!

Patrick Daley

A: First I take the skull. I make a sculpture of it. Then I figure out what the face on the sculpture might be.

Q: So you actually handle the skulls?

A: Sure. It's the only way I can make a lifelike head.

Q: What else do you do?

A: I "age" criminals for the police and the FBI. Let's say that the police are looking for someone who disappeared many years ago. The guy has gotten older. He looks different. I look at an old picture. Then I create a sculpture of what he probably looks like now.

Q: Does it work?

A: Oh, yeah! I've helped catch seven criminals.

Q: So you started as an artist. How did you get into this work?

A: I was taking art courses in Philadelphia. I wanted to be a better artist. I knew I had to learn more about the human body.

Q: So what did you do?

A: A friend of mine works at a morgue. That's where they keep dead bodies. So he showed me all these bodies. Some had been in bad accidents. Some had died violently. This one woman only had a number. He said to me, we don't know her name or what she looks like.

Q: How awful! What happened then?

A: I told him that I could show him what she looked like. So I came in the next night. I got the body out of the freezer.

I took some measurements. Then I did a sculpture. Five months later, the police found out who she was. Twenty years later—just last year—they caught the man who killed her. So the family came over and thanked me. What a good feeling that was!

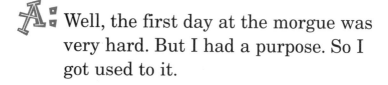 Still, most of the people you deal with are dead. How did you get used to that?

Well, the first day at the morgue was very hard. But I had a purpose. So I got used to it.

I'm not so sure I would get used to it so quickly! Anyway, tell me what you're doing today.

The police dropped a skull off at my studio earlier this week. I've been studying it. I try to figure out what makes this person different from everyone else. Then I put the clay on

America's Most Wanted

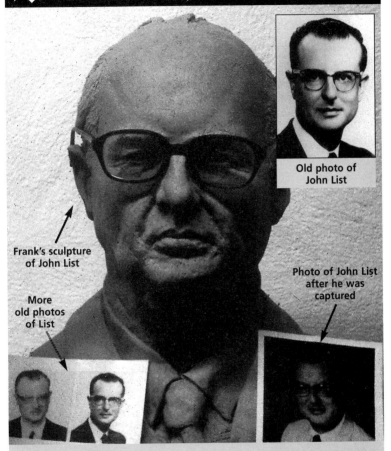

Old photo of
John List

Frank's sculpture
of John List

Photo of John List
after he was
captured

More
old photos
of List

In 1989, producers of the show "America's Most Wanted" came to Frank. They had old photos of a murderer named John List. List had been missing for 18 years.

The producers wanted Frank to make a sculpture showing what List looks like now. Frank did. The sculpture was shown on TV. Eleven days later, List was found!

and shape the face. I usually sculpt the hair, too. The police won't pay for a good wig. And I don't want to use a bad one.

Q: How do you get the hair right?

A: You look at the face and you think like a hairdresser. You ask, what type of hairstyle would go with this face? In many cases I come pretty close.

Q: So then you make a mold around the whole thing?

A: Exactly, and I pour a chemical into it. It hardens. Then I sand it and fine-tune it. Then I paint it.

Q: How long does this whole process take?

A: About a month.

Q: That's a pretty long time. Do you start to feel like you know this person?

A: Sure. You have to get to know the person. Often I dream about them. Say I'm working on a criminal. I put myself in his mind. I try to feel what he might be feeling.

Q: Wow! So are you always thinking about your work?

A: In a way. I'm a people person. I love looking at people. No matter where I am, I'm studying faces.

The Skull Man at Work

Frank's work starts when the police have a skull they cannot identify. They hand it over to Frank. He gets to work. The process of making the sculpture takes about a month. Here are some of the steps along the way.

1 Frank starts by getting a feel for the skull. He studies it. He measures it. Then he's ready for the next step.

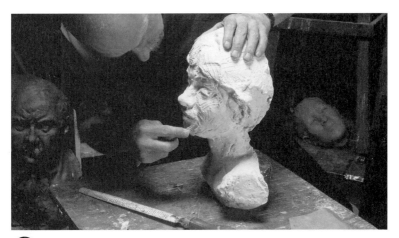

2 What did this skull look like with skin and flesh? Frank finds out by building up the face with clay. Then he makes a mold of this head. And he fills the mold with a chemical that hardens.

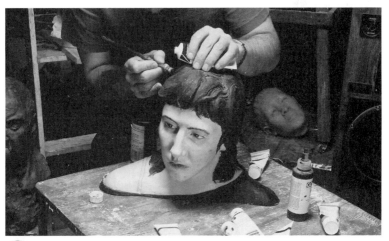

3 Then the head is ready for the finishing touches. Skin tones are added. Lips and eyes are painted. Frank adds hair he has made. Now the skull is ready for the police.

Amy Weller

Do you like ice cream? Do you like it *a lot?* Would you want to spend every day around ice cream?

That's what Amy Weller does. She works in an ice cream factory. In fact, she works for the king of ice cream makers, Ben and Jerry. She's a tour guide at their ice cream factory in Waterbury, Vermont.

Some people say that the tour at Ben & Jerry's is the most popular factory tour in the country. Maybe that's because at the end of it, tourists get their fill of free ice cream. Now, how cool is that!?

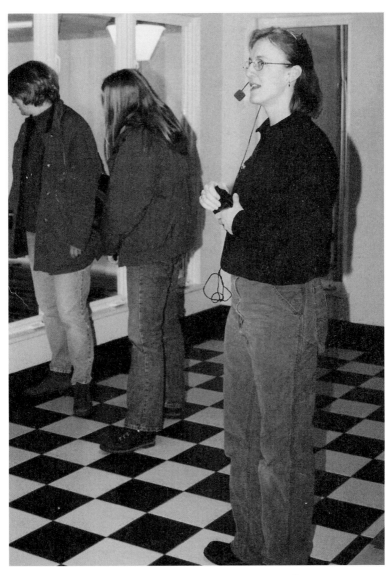

Amy Weller shows some visitors around Ben & Jerry's ice cream factory.

Q: First, I need to know something. Do you get free ice cream?

A: Oh, sure—plenty of it! All workers at Ben & Jerry's get to take home three pints a day. We can have any flavor we like.

Q: Wow, three pints a day sounds like a lot. Can you eat that much?

A: Oh, I have kids at home who are very happy to help. And neighbors, too! But you'd be surprised. I don't eat that much ice cream any more!

Q: Do you have to love ice cream to be a tour guide for Ben & Jerry's?

A: It helps. Actually, we have some people working here who don't eat ice cream. But that's okay—you don't have to like ice cream to still like the company.

Q: One magazine said that the Ben & Jerry's tour was one of the top tours in America. Why is it so much fun?

A: We take you through the whole ice cream-making process. You see cows hanging out outside the factory. Then

Here's where it all starts! Cows provide the main ingredients for ice cream—milk and cream. They're so good at their work that Ben and Jerry call them "living machines."

you go to a room that looks like a barn. Next, we take you into a room where the ice cream is made. You see huge buckets of ice cream.

Q: Is there a lot of ice cream in that room?

A: There's probably more ice cream there than anyone could eat in their whole life!

Q: Has anything ever gone wrong during a tour?

A: Sure. Once a huge bucket of ice cream had a leak. There was a flood of vanilla ice cream all over the place. People loved that!

Q: How does a tour usually end?

A: We give out two scoops of ice cream to everyone. That's a pretty good ending.

This is the production room. It's where fruit, candy, and other good stuff is mixed into the ice cream. The ice cream is also frozen here.

Ben & Jerry's ice cream trucks take ice cream to all 50 states. The ice cream is also sold in Canada and Europe. The company sells about $60 million worth of ice cream a year!

Q: Is it hard to keep people's attention during the tour when they know there is ice cream waiting for them?

A: This may surprise you, but kids pay attention all the way through the tour.

It's the adults who want to skip right to the ice cream!

Q: Does it take a lot of training to be a tour guide?

A: There are two hard weeks of training. We have to be able to answer any question. We have to know everything— from ice cream-making to Ben and Jerry's shirt sizes. We also have to know everything about every single flavor.

Q: So you can list all the flavors?

A: You bet! Go ahead, test me.

Q: Okay, what's in the flavor Wavy Gravy?

A: That's the toughest. Okay, it's caramel, cashew, and Brazil nut ice cream. It also has a chocolate hazelnut fudge swirl and almonds.

Q: That's pretty good. Do people often ask you to name the flavors?

A: All the time. Sometimes we have fun with them. We have a very popular flavor called Phish Food. It's named after the rock band Phish. People ask us what's in it. We tell them it is halibut-based, with chunks of cod. Get it?

Q: Yeah, I get it: *Phish* sounds like *fish*. Yuck! So, what's the silliest question you've ever heard?

A: Hmm . . . probably, "When does the 12:00 o'clock tour start?" You have to stop yourself from answering, "Duh!" Also, everyone asks if Ben and Jerry are real—and if they are still alive. Tell your readers that, yes, they are alive and well.

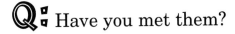 Have you met them?

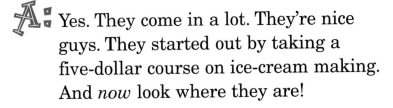 Yes. They come in a lot. They're nice guys. They started out by taking a five-dollar course on ice-cream making. And *now* look where they are!

Q: Look where *you* are. Is this job as much fun as it sounds?

A: More! If a kid falls down and scrapes his knee, we give him some ice cream. If he drops his cone, we give him more ice cream. It's hard to have a bad day around here.

Jorge Ramos

Do you like to ride trains or subways? Got any ideas for building a better train or subway station? Could you handle hanging out underground?

If so, you might want to check out Jorge Ramos's job. Jorge spends a lot of time under the streets of New York City. That's because he's fixing part of the subway.

A subway is a system of trains that run underground. New York City has one of the busiest subways in the world. Millions of people ride it each day. And it's about 100 years old! So, how do you improve something so big, busy, and old? Let's find out!

Q: First, there's one question that I have to ask. . . .

A: Wait! I know what the question is. And the answer is YES! I do ride the subway. It's fast. It's fun. It's the best way to get around. I love being in a subway train!

Jorge Ramos looks over his plans to improve a subway station.

Q: Okay. So what kind of work does an architect like you do?

A: I draw plans for buildings, homes, and even subway stations.

Q: Have you always liked to draw?

A: Yes. I grew up in Columbia, in South America. As a boy, I drew pictures of the beautiful buildings in my country. I thought some day I would draw pictures for magazines and books. But when I moved to the United States, I became interested in subway stations.

Q: Really? Why are you so interested in subway stations?

A: It's a big challenge to design a space that millions of people use each day. It's got to be easy for people to figure out where they're going. And the space must be easy for people to move around in. You don't want them bumping into each other or plowing each other down! Also, the space has to look good, and be safe.

Q: Tell me about the project you're working on right now.

A: We are fixing up a subway station in a part of New York City called Queens.

Q: What's the first thing you did to get that project started?

A: I had a big meeting. I asked people from the neighborhood how they thought their subway station could be improved.

Q: What was that meeting like?

A: It was loud! Everyone had an opinion. In fact, you'd be surprised how many opinions there were at that meeting.

Q: Oh yeah? Like what?

A: Some people wanted a bigger station. Some people thought the station was too big. Some people wanted the station to be cleaner. Some wanted it to be safer. Some people thought that the station needed murals and other kinds of art.

Q: Did you start building the station right after the meeting?

Jorge's station is just one part of New York City's huge subway system. There are about 700 miles of tracks. And more than one billion people ride the rails each year!

A: No. I began planning *how* to build it. I met with builders. I met with people who work for the subway system. Then I took my plans back to the neighborhood.

Q: Why would you go back to another meeting? The first one sounded awful!

A: Well, it wasn't really so awful—just noisy and busy. Plus, I really want people in the neighborhood to be a part of the planning. After all, it really is *their* subway station.

Q: After all of that, the building part must be easy, right?

A: Are you kidding? Working on a subway station is never easy. Here's why: We can't close the subway station during the day. So we have to work late at night. Also, we can't work in bad weather. So forget about getting much done in the winter.

Q: What's left to do at the station you're building now?

A: I have to make sure that the subway signs are clear and helpful. So I'll test them first. I'll make a bunch of paper signs. Then I'll go to the station and tape them up. I'll pretend that I am a visitor. Can I find my way around? Or do I get lost? I'll take a lot of notes about what happens. After that test, I'll make changes to the signs. Then the paper signs will be made into real signs.

Q: What else have you done to help visitors in the station?

A: There is a law that says we must put ramps and elevators in all stations. That way, elderly people and people in wheelchairs can ride the subway. Next to the tracks where the trains come, we paint the floor with a special paint. The paint has tiny bumps in it. The bumps let blind people know when they are standing too close to the train tracks.

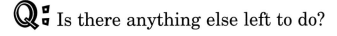 Is there anything else left to do?

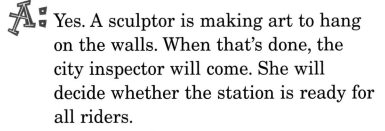 Yes. A sculptor is making art to hang on the walls. When that's done, the city inspector will come. She will decide whether the station is ready for all riders.

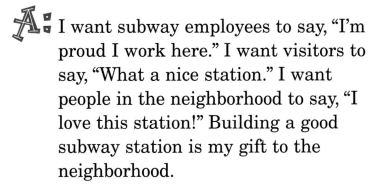 What do you want people to say about the new station?

I want subway employees to say, "I'm proud I work here." I want visitors to say, "What a nice station." I want people in the neighborhood to say, "I love this station!" Building a good subway station is my gift to the neighborhood.

Bruce Thorson

Sports Photographer

Are you into sports? Do you check out the sports pages of the local paper? When you're channel surfing, do you often stop at ESPN?

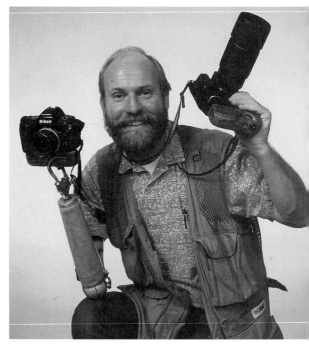

Bruce always travels with a bagful of cameras . . . and a lot of film.

34

If you answered yes to any of these questions, you might enjoy a job like Bruce Thorson's. Bruce is a sports photographer. He uses pictures to help writers and reporters tell about a game.

Q: Okay Bruce, tell me what you do exactly.

A: I'm a sports photographer. My job is to take pictures at games and sports events. The pictures are then used in the newspaper.

Q: Does that mean you get to go to a million sports events?

A: I don't go to a *million* games and events. But I sure go to a lot of them!

Q: Wow! That sounds pretty cool. Is it hard to be a sports photographer?

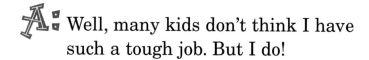 Well, many kids don't think I have such a tough job. But I do!

Q: What do you mean?

A: Just imagine. I'm out covering a big game. The whole town is waiting to read about it the next day. What do you think happens if I don't get a good shot?

Q: I don't know. What?

A: Well, it makes problems for a lot of people. The writer will have a tough time telling the story. The readers don't get to see a great picture. It hurts the newspaper, too. If another paper has better photos, people may start buying that paper instead!

Q: Okay, so tell me how good sports photographers do their jobs.

A: First I meet with the sports writers.

I listen to their plans. They tell me what events they want to write about.

Q: Then what happens?

A: I pack my bags. I check to make sure I have enough film and all the lenses that I'll need. Then I grab a map. There are a lot of schools and sports teams in this area. I need to make sure I get to the right one. And I have to be on time.

Q: How many pictures will you take?

A: Lots! I take many pictures of the game. I take a lot of close-up pictures, too. Sometimes I will just follow one athlete and take lots of pictures of him or her. I also take pictures of the fans.

Q: Why would a sports photographer take pictures of fans?

A: Sometimes the faces of fans really

show victory or defeat. Besides, there's nothing better than a picture of a fan who is very happy about something that has just happened on the court or field.

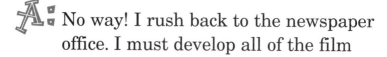 When the game is over, are you done for the day?

No way! I rush back to the newspaper office. I must develop all of the film

Bruce has to get just the right shot to help the writer tell a good story.

myself. You don't think I drop it off at an overnight developer do you!?

Q: No, I guess not. What happens next?

A: I look closely at every picture. As soon as I have picked my favorite ones, I rush over to the writers. They're waiting for the photos. Photos help them write good stories.

Q: What are your favorite sports to photograph?

A: I love basketball the best. It's fast and exciting. I love to hear the roar of the crowd. I love to listen to the coaches and the players. I like baseball, too. It's fun to watch the catchers tease the batters.

Q: As a photographer, what other sports do you like?

A: I like track events. These athletes race against each other and against time. You never know when a new record will be set. There is a lot of feeling on the faces of these athletes.

Q: What is the hardest part about being a photographer?

A: Sometimes it is very crowded at a big game. People will bump into my camera. They'll get in the way of a really great shot.

Q: Many kids will read this book. What can they do if they want to be a sports photographer?

A: There are a lot of things kids can do. Here are some:
- Practice taking pictures at games and sporting events.
- Cut out great sports photos from magazines and newspapers.
- Try writing your own story about a game. That will help you see what kinds of photos you need.

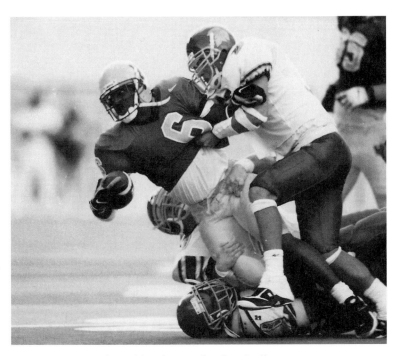

Bruce shot this photo of a football game in Portland, Oregon.

Q: Do you have any other tips?

A: Yes. Don't forget to take the lens cap off of your camera. That can be a big mistake! Trust me, I know!

Michelle Gaffney

Do you love animals? All kinds of animals? What about big animals, like the ones you might find in Africa? Do you think you could handle feeding them? Washing them? Making sure they are healthy?

If so, Michelle Gaffney's job might be right for you. Michelle is an animal keeper. She works for the Wild Animal Park in San Diego, California. People come from all over to see and study the animals that live there.

Q: As an animal keeper, what exactly is your job?

A: It's my job to keep the animals happy and safe.

Michelle has to stand on a jeep to feed this giraffe.
Giraffes are the tallest animals in the world. Some of
them are 17 feet tall!

Q: Do you work with all the animals in the park?

A: I work with the animals that come from Africa and East Asia. I work with rhinos, giraffes, zebras, and gazelles.

Q: Why do you work with animals from these countries?

A: It's because of the way our park is set up. Animals that live near each other in the wild are kept together in the park. We want the animals' homes in the park to be as much like their natural homes as possible.

Q: How does your day begin?

A: Well, I'll tell you one thing—it begins too early! I get up at five o'clock. I eat breakfast. I put on my uniform. Then it's time to head to the park.

Q: What happens next?

A: I load my truck with food for the animals. Here at the park, we use food that the animals would eat in the wild. My animals are plant eaters. You wouldn't think that leaves and grass and crumbs could weigh so much!

Q: Then do you get to take a break?

Most zebras come from southern or eastern Africa. They're related to horses, but they're smaller. They have more stripes, too!

A waterbuck looks over Michelle's shoulder.

A: No! I drive to the animals' homes and feed them.

Q: What do you do when feeding time is over?

A: First, we go around and count all the animals. We make sure that each one is okay. Most of the time, they all are. Sometimes we will bring a sick animal to the vet. Sometimes a pregnant giraffe, or zebra, or gazelle will go off somewhere to have her babies. Then we must go looking for her. Finding her babies is another story.

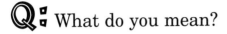 What do you mean?

Well, after the mothers have their babies, they hide them. They're trying to protect them. We have to climb high up into the hills and look behind rocks. We have to look under fallen tree limbs. We keep looking until we spot them. It can really take a long time.

Do the mothers want you to be near the babies?

Not really. But, we need to make sure the babies are okay. We don't get too close unless we have to. For instance, if a baby looks too small, we bring it in and weigh it.

What other jobs do you do?

A: I have many other jobs. Some animals might need shots. Others might need to be washed or combed. And some of the rhinos may need to have their toenails clipped.

Q: What? Are you kidding? You don't really clip the rhinos' toenails, do you?

A: Sure! I know it sounds crazy, but it's really one of my favorite jobs. First, I bring the rhino something he loves— a big bucket of sweet grass, seeds, and crumbs. Then I rub his belly. Soon he will roll over—just like a puppy. Then I take a pair of giant clippers and slowly begin to clip his toenails. If I'm lucky he'll let me work on him for almost an hour.

Q: You must really love animals to do that! Have you always loved animals?

A: Always, always, always! When I was a kid, I thought I'd be a vet some day.

Michelle feeds an Indian rhino. Her next job?
Clipping its toenails!

Did you like this book?

Here are two other READ 180 Paperbacks that you might like to read.

Let's Go Surfing: An Internet Adventure

Do you need some information? And fast? This book tells you how to log onto the Internet and find what you need!

By John DiConsiglio
With an Internet guide by Francie Alexander and Nancy Hechinger

Animal E.R.

A group of kids have won a contest. The prize? A day at the local animal hospital. You'll go with them as they help take care of a dog, a cat, a snake, a monkey, an iguana, and even a gorilla!

By Jordan Brown

Glossary

athlete	someone who is trained in, or very good at, sports or games that require strength, speed, and/or skill
chemical	a solid, liquid, or gas that can be mixed with other stuff to form a reaction or make a change
cod	a kind of fish
criminals	people who commit a crime
describe	create a picture of something in words
develop	In this book, it means to treat film with chemicals to bring out the pictures that have been taken.
developer	In this book, it means someone who develops film.
emotional	having to do with your feelings

entertain	to amuse and interest someone
gazelles	graceful antelopes found in Africa and Asia
halibut	a type of fish
hazelnut	a kind of nut
improved	made better
inspector	someone who inspects or examines things
lenses	In this book, it means the piece of curved glass or plastic that can be attached to a camera. Lenses can help photographers get close-up shots.
limbs	In this book, it means the branches of a tree.
measurements	size or weight of something
mold	In this book, it means a hollow container that you can pour liquid into, so that it sets into that shape.

morgue	a place where dead bodies are kept
murals	paintings on a wall
opinion	an idea or belief that you have about something
photographer	a person who takes photos
pints	a unit of measurement equal to half a quart
pregnant	expecting a baby
process	an organized series of actions that produce a result
respect	admire and have a high opinion of
rhinos	rhinoceroses; animals from Africa and Asia that have thick skin and one or two large horns on their noses
sculpture	something carved or shaped out of stone, wood, metal, marble, or clay or cast in bronze or another metal

subway	a system of trains that run mostly underground
tease	to playfully make fun of someone
tour	a trip, often for sightseeing
tourists	people who travel and visit places for fun
victory	a win in a battle, contest, or game
violently	done with extreme force
zebra	a wild animal of southern and eastern Africa, that looks like a horse, except that it is smaller and has black and white stripes